Copyright © 2020 Prof Claudia Gray & Sarita Kruger

All rights reserved. This book or any portion thereof may not be reproduced or used in any manner whatsoever without the express written permission of the publisher except for the use of brief quotations in a book review.

First printed 2020

ISBN 978-1-77629-108-3

Danny goes to BIG SCHOOL

Written by Paediatrician
Prof Claudia Gray

Illustrated by
Sarita Kruger

"...That you're in!
You can go there!
You'll be an "Oak" lad,
With a green and blue
uniform, just like your Dad!"

I play and I sing and
they're teaching me how
To make letters from playdough
and shapes in the mud...

"But Danny," said mum,
"you are constantly growing
And the rule is that when
you turn 6 you are going
To Grade 1, and that means
a new school must arrive,

As Acorns is only for age three to five.

And big school will teach about writing and reading
And playing in a team and about following and leading.

By the end of each year when you've written and read, You'll be perfectly ready for the next year ahead."

All holiday Dan thought about the new school, Which felt scary and big with a uniform rule.

And perhaps when you're six there'd be no time to play And they'd make you sit upright to study all day?

There would be no nice Tom, would he make a new friend? Oh why did his time at Acorn have to end?!

Just like that the big morning of Big School was there. Mum helped with the uniform, tidied his hair...

...And gave him his backpack with lunchbox inside; Then Dad took a photograph, beaming with pride.

"Hello, is this Danny?" asked the man at the boom
As he smiled and took Dan to a splendid big room,

Filled with happily chattering uniformed boys
And -wow- they were playing with all sorts of toys!

And then happily off to the playground he ran...

Then sit in a circle, don't wriggle or roam;
For straight after this story you'll be fetched to go home."

Back with mum in the car
Danny told her with glee
How they sang about seeds
growing into a tree.

"Do you know mum, said Dan, "what will happen to me?

My roots will grow strong and my shoots will grow free.

Yes mummy, how big and strong one day I'll be: Just like an Acorn becomes an Oak tree."

...of Oak boys who could count, read and write.

LET'S REVISE SOME KEY CONCEPTS IN THE BOOK:
Types of Schools

Nursery school (also called pre-primary school or Kindergarten)

This is where the younger children start off. They learn to make friends, and play so very much. They draw and paint and sing and jump. We can learn so much through play!

Primary school

Primary school usually starts at around age 6 and is a time when children build further on what they have learned at nursery school, but still in a fun way! At primary school children learn to read books, to write letters and even sentences and to count. As they go further down the years in primary school, children even learn to read difficult books with jolly many pages and small print. They learn all sorts of complicated sums (maths) and can even write interesting stories themselves!

High school

Wow, high school is for really big children, usually from about 13 years of age. High school children learn super hard stuff- but remember- their primary school years have prepared them for this! By the end of high school, children have to write mega-important tests, which make them ready for university or college.

Colleges and Universities

Young adults choose what they want to do as a job and study towards this at colleges or universities. There are many, many jobs to choose from- teachers, police-workers, doctors, nurses, business-people, engineers, astronauts, artists and so many more! Why don't you ask your parents what they studied towards? Did it take them a long time?

The classroom

The classroom at school is where children spend most of their inside-time. Here, they play or they sit at their desks and draw and write and read and learn. Don't worry- at the start of big school there will still be plenty of time for play!

The playground

At school, there will be regular breaks for play time! If the weather is good, children at school can play on the playground. There may be slides and jungle-gyms and swings. Remember to give each other turns on all the play-things, trying to share nicely. This is not always easy! Please tell your teacher straightaway if you are hurt on the playground or if someone is playing very rough.

The library

The library at school is a wonderful place filled with books of all shapes and sizes! The library teacher often reads to children in the library and may even give the children books to take home for a few days. Please remember to look after the library books and to bring them back at the right time!

The school hall

Many schools have a big room called a "hall," where children from many classes may get together for singing or for an "assembly," when the teachers may have some very important messages to tell you. Try to be quiet when it is hall time- it is very hard for a teacher to speak to so many children if it is very noisy!

Circle time

Especially during the first few years of life, many classes have circle time, when the children need to sit still in a special spot, sometimes in a big circle, to listen to the teacher, who tells them about all sorts of things. The teacher may ask the children questions- remember to answer when it is your turn- and not to be scared- this is all about learning. Often during circle time the teacher will read a lovely story, or sing a song with the children. Even though you may feel like wriggling a lot during circle time, try to sit still, then you will learn so much!

As a young child, Claudia used to write stories for her little cousins and dreamed of becoming a "professional babysitter." Her love for children converted itself into a career as a Paediatrician, trained both in the UK and in South Africa. Claudia's life is full-to-the-brim with a busy career and 4 cherished children, which sidelined her writing career for many years. Finally, she has now had the opportunity, together with the talented Sarita as illustrator, to write a series of childrens' stories which aim to take scary situations and explain them in a fun and reassuring way.

Sarita is also a mom of 2 with a passion for design and communication. She is excited about this opportunity to visually relay Claudia's messages and reduce stress for little people.

"Our children are our greatest treasure. They are our future.
The true character of a society is revealed in how it treats its children."
Nelson Mandela

www.ingramcontent.com/pod-product-compliance
Lightning Source LLC
Chambersburg PA
CBHW051120110526
44589CB00026B/2990